How to Draw
Deltora
Dragons
and Other Creatures

Marc McBride
with
Emily Rodda

SCHOLASTIC INC.

New York Toronto London Auckland Sydney
Mexico City New Delhi Hong Kong Buenos Aires

For Sofie
MM

ISBN-13: 978-0-439-91298-3
ISBN-10: 0-439-91298-9

12 11 10 9 8 7 6 5 4 3 2   7 8 9 10 11 12/0

Printed in the U.S.A.   40

First Scholastic paperback printing, February 2007

Designed by Simone Kelleher

Typeset in Berkeley

Contents

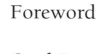

Foreword

In this book, Marc McBride reveals more of his drawing secrets, and helps us all to understand how he brings to life in pictures the dragons and other beings which inhabit the land of Deltora. I am sure that Deltora fans, and all lovers of fantasy who enjoy illustration, will welcome this chance to develop their drawing skills by following Marc's advice. You couldn't have a better teacher!

Emily Rodda

Emily Rodda

We all need inspiration to create art, and the world of nature is the best place to find inspiration. Look at the twisting branches of a tree and you might get ideas for what an alien might look like, or the patterns on a leaf for the wings of a dragon, and I'm sure we have all seen amazing things in clouds!

I have created more than one hundred and fifty book covers, but my favorites are those for the Deltora Quest books, and I think I know why. My inspiration came from Emily Rodda's wonderful stories, as well as from the drawings children around the world send me, based on my own drawings. Illustrators spend most of their time alone drawing, never really knowing if anyone likes their work, so it is a huge thrill to find out when people do. In return, I wanted to create this new book on how to draw my favorite things—Dragons.

I really like to draw in a museum that has dinosaur bones on display. There I can learn about the shape and structure of these great dragon-like beasts, but because no one knows what patterns, colors or spines they had, I can have fun making them up. Dragons, perhaps the mightiest of all beasts, would have no need for camouflage—they wouldn't need to hide from anything. I give mine great bright patterns in their scales and lots of spines. l love the Chinese dragons that represent good luck, and the majestic European dragons that brave warriors battle in an attempt to rescue the princess. Just remember the underbelly of Deltora dragons changes to match the color of the sky and make the flames the same color as the dragon.

I've also included some other popular creatures and characters from the land of Deltora. You can combine these in various drawings just as I have done in this book. Happy drawing!

Marc McBride

Opal Dragon

The Opal Dragon is the largest of Deltora's Dragons. Its scales shine with all the colors of the rainbow. Its gem is the symbol of hope, and its territory is in the center of Deltora, in the land of the Plains.

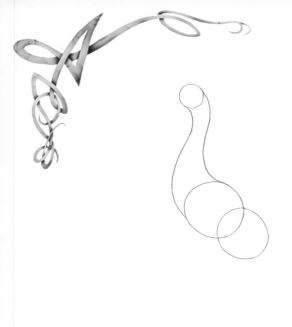

1. Draw two circles, one slightly bigger that the other. Add a much smaller circle above them. Join the lines to form the long neck tapering in to meet the head circle.

2. Add two giant wings. The one on the right passes through the lowest circle.

3. Add a "snout" to the head circle. Join the body circles and add a curling tail.

4. Draw a line in the middle of the snout for a mouth. Add two arms and a claw at the bottom of the larger wing. Add a small flap at the top of this wing and a thin cylindrical shape joining it to the body.

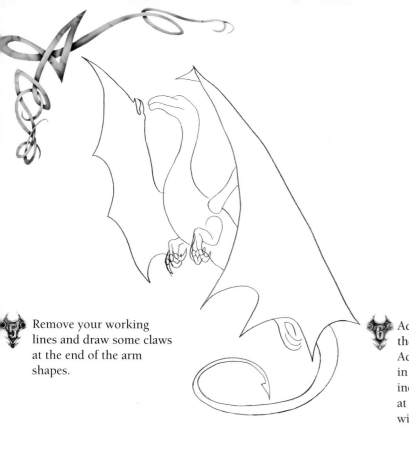

5. Remove your working lines and draw some claws at the end of the arm shapes.

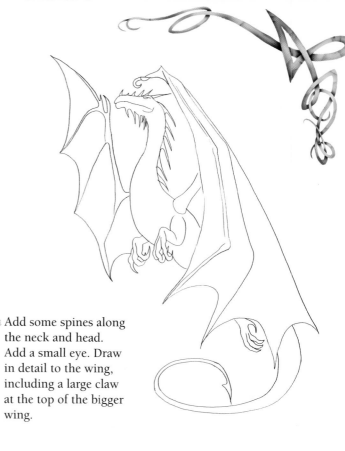

6. Add some spines along the neck and head. Add a small eye. Draw in detail to the wing, including a large claw at the top of the bigger wing.

7. Add some pattern to the dragon, using the lines to show their vast size, and add some mountains in the distance.

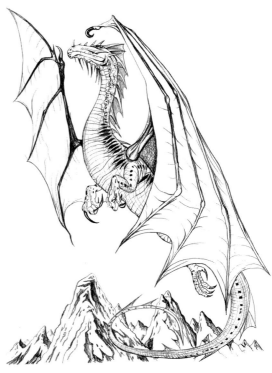

8. Add shading over the pattern lines you have drawn—inside the wings will be the darkest. Add shading to the mountains. Make sure the shadows are all on the same side.

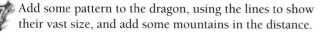

Diamond Dragon

This newly hatched Diamond Dragon is small enough to fit into a human's pocket, and its scales are far softer than the scales of an adult. It grows very fast, however, and its wings are soon strong enough to fly.

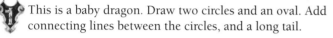 This is a baby dragon. Draw two circles and an oval. Add connecting lines between the circles, and a long tail.

Draw the dragon's head with hooks on each beak. Begin drawing an arm inside the larger circle, and add a half-oval shape on the lower side of the neck. Draw a line from the oval shape to follow the curling tail.

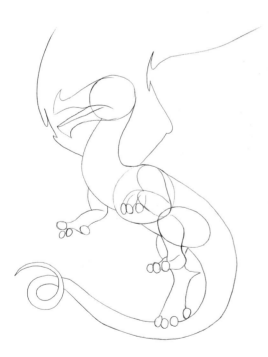

Start drawing in the arms, legs, hands and feet using small circles for the knuckles. Note how the back leg behind the body stretches downwards. Begin the shapes for the wings.

Finish the wing shapes and the fingers, adding long triangular shapes for the claws. Give the baby dragon a big eye inside the head circle.

 Rub out your working lines. Make sure the lines are clean. Start adding details to the wings, and draw spines on the tail. Draw in some teeth and some punk-like spines to the head.

 Add patterns to the skin—think of animals and fish or lizard scales.

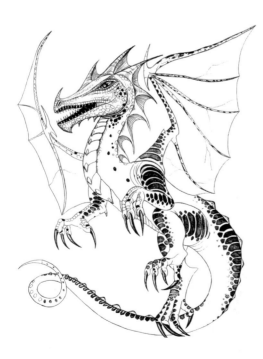

 Color in your pattern. Draw in some scales—you can be as intricate as you like.

Start shading over the pattern with a soft pencil (4B is good). Remember, the sunlight comes from above, so make the shading darker under the wings, arms, legs and head.

Ruby Dragon

The Ruby Dragon lives in Deltora's east. It has been accused of savagery but is, in fact, a placid beast, unless it is attacked or threatened. Its gem is the symbol of happiness.

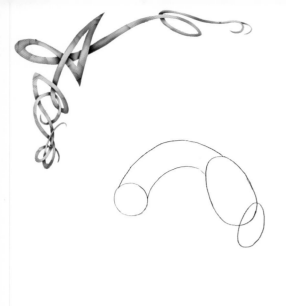

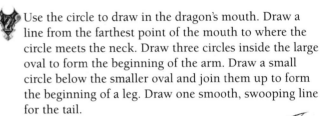

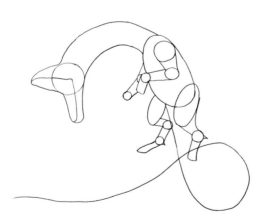

Draw two ovals with a circle to the left of them. Join the circle to the left-hand oval with two arch shapes to form the neck.

Use the circle to draw in the dragon's mouth. Draw a line from the farthest point of the mouth to where the circle meets the neck. Draw three circles inside the large oval to form the beginning of the arm. Draw a small circle below the smaller oval and join them up to form the beginning of a leg. Draw one smooth, swooping line for the tail.

Start drawing the other arm and leg. They are behind the body and further away, so they will be smaller than the ones you have already drawn. Add simple rectangular shapes for the feet and claws.

Starting where the neck and large oval meet, draw a wing shape. Allow your line to get closer to the tail line, and follow it along and eventually join it at the end so the wing is joined to the tail.

Start drawing another wing behind the first one. Draw triangle shapes for the teeth and claws, and another triangle at the end of the tail. Add an eye inside the head circle and a nostril outside it.

Draw in the rest of the second wing. Add spines around the head and an extra bit of skin on the wing where it bends. Don't forget to draw in some flames.

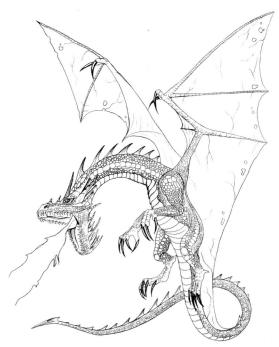

Rub out your working lines. We now have the main shape of the dragon and can start adding the detail. Mine is a bit battle-weary, so it has holes in its wings.

Finally, add a pattern before you add shading. Remember that light usually comes from above so the bottom parts of the dragon will be darker.

Emerald Dragon

The Emerald Dragon guards the territory of the Dread Gnomes. Its gem is the symbol of honor, and it is the sternest of all Deltora's dragons.

1 Draw two circles that just touch, one bigger than the other. Add a smaller circle above them. Join the circles with connecting lines and allow the lines to curl below to form a long tail.

2 Draw more circles as shown. Draw the two shapes to form the outline of an open mouth.

3 Join each circle to the one next to it to form the arms and legs. Add some spines to the head and give your dragon a large wing.

4 Add claws to the arms and legs using small circles for knuckles. Add some detail into the wing and draw a second wing behind it.

 Add a line below the top part of the mouth and add a row of teeth to both jaws. Add an eye, a nostril and more spines from the face. Divide the neck into two. Add more detail into the wings, with a couple of claws mid-wing and a triangular spike on the tail.

 Remove all your working lines and add detail into the remaining lines. I've given the wings of my dragon a more jagged, battle-worn look. Add spines from the top of the neck along the tail.

Draw on a pattern of reptile scales. You can draw just a few to save time.

Decide where your light source is and start shading the parts further away from the light. Use the side of your pencil lead (4B is good for this).

Topaz Dragon

This golden dragon, whose gem is the symbol of faith, lives in the territory of Del.
Its lair is in the Os-Mine Hills, where it preys on the beasts called Granous.

Here's a dragon that you can draw on your own. The stages are similar to the ones you've already done.

The Fear

The Fear is a terrible beast which lives in a cave in the secret sea beneath Deltora. For centuries it has terrorized the Plume tribe, demanding a living sacrifice each year. In the center of its body is a tearing beak, and its ten huge tentacles are tipped with stinging white threads.

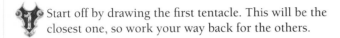

1 Start off by drawing the first tentacle. This will be the closest one, so work your way back for the others.

2 Draw two more tentacles on either side of the first one.

3 Draw three more twisting tentacles behind the first three.

4 Now draw a tentacle reaching upwards in the center of the ones you've already drawn, then draw another twisting one next to it.

5 Draw another twisting tentacle below the last one, then draw an arching tentacle in the background.

6 Draw in the suckers on the underside of the tentacles—lots of simple oval shapes with a smaller oval inside them.

7 Draw some thin "fingers" at the end of each of the ten tentacles. Give your Fear a pattern—mine is snake-like.

8 Start shading with a soft pencil. Remember that the underside of your creature will be the darkest as the light source is coming from above. Each sucker will also have a shadow under it.

Arach

Arach lurk on rafts of web which float on the waters of the secret sea beneath Deltora. Their bodies are covered with a glossy black shell, as though plated with armor. They like dark, warm places, and fear the light.

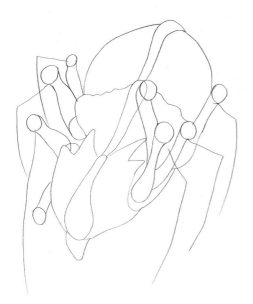

Draw the torso of the spider-like creature. It is roughly three sections with a head.

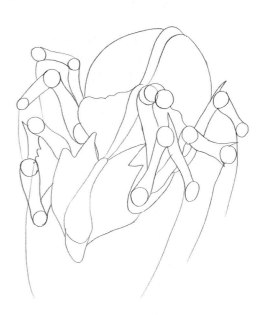

Think about how a large spider walks, then draw in lines to start six of the eight legs.

Draw a small circle at the first angle of each leg line. Draw a line from the other side of the circle to join the main body.

Draw another circle at the next angle of the leg lines. Join these to the previous circles and add spines.

5 Finish the detail of the legs, adding some sharp points. Add some jagged lines to the back legs. Add some fangs to the mouth.

6 Add some jagged lines to the legs and get rid of all the working lines.

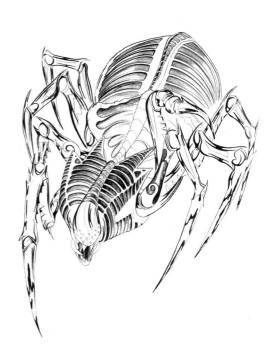

7 Add some pattern to give it a skeletal appearance with some jagged lines around the legs. Add lots of little eyes.

8 Shade in the patterns. Add some strong reflections—this creature is black and shiny. Finish it with shading over the top.

The Kobb

The Kobb is one of the most fearsome beasts to be found in Deltora's seas.
When hunting for prey, it floats on the surface of the water, so that it looks like a mat of seaweed.
Its lair is always on land—usually an island, which it covers with its slime.

1. First draw a circle, then draw more circles behind it, making them smaller as they go back. Only show the parts of these circles that would not be hidden by those in front.

2. Draw a big gaping mouth in the first circle and a fish-like tail on the end of the last circle.

3. Draw an arch inside the mouth for the creature's throat and a large protruding tongue. Add a flipper and the kelp-like whiskers. Don't forget to add the small deadly eye just behind the open mouth.

4. Add detail to the kelp-like whiskers. Add two nostrils and the razor-sharp teeth.

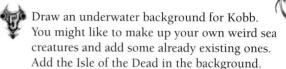 Draw an underwater background for Kobb. You might like to make up your own weird sea creatures and add some already existing ones. Add the Isle of the Dead in the background.

 Shade your drawing with a soft (at least 2B) pencil. I used a 4B for mine. (This is much faster than using an HB although the lead breaks much more easily, so be careful!)

For underwater scenes, remember that the light comes from above, so the underside of all your creatures will be darker and the scene should get darker the deeper you go. You might want to add rays of light using a ruler. I've added Kobb's shadow on the seaweedy floor in my finished drawing.

Adin and the Belt of Deltora

Adin the blacksmith created the Belt of Deltora. He persuaded the seven tribes of the land to unite. He led the tribes in battle to defeat the Shadow Lord, and became Deltora's first king.

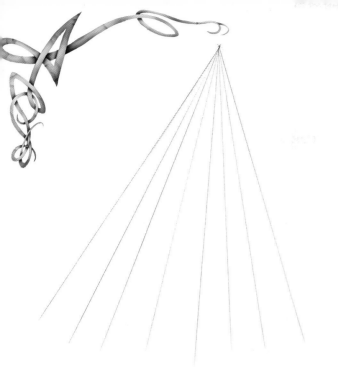

1 Draw an X toward the top of the page. Draw several lines from the bottom of the page that meet at the X.

2 Draw a circle a short distance below the X. Draw a curved line below the circle and another line curving in the opposite direction toward the bottom of the page. Draw a third curved line roughly one-third down from the top line.

3 Join the circle to the top curved line and draw a triangle below it. Draw another line above the middle curved line. Begin to draw two large boots above the bottom curved line. Draw two wavy lines above the boots for the bottom edge of the cloak.

4 Join the boots to the cloak and continue toward the belt. Draw a wavy line from the inner edges of the cloak to the edge of the triangle. Draw a line from the center of the triangle to the middle curved line (the belt). Rub out the bottom of the circle and divide the face into three. Draw a simple hand shape from the edge of the cloak to the belt.

 Add some eyes below the top line in the head, a nose above the middle line and a mouth below that. Begin adding detail to the hand and add gems to the belt. Add heels to the boots—the boots are closer to us, so add more detail.

 Add hair framing the face. Start drawing folds in the clothes and boots. For the checkered floor, imagine a vanishing point X further down and draw the lines from this X.

Start shading. Because we are looking up at the figure we can see the underside of the chin, which is dark. Also, there are lots of shadows from the long cloak. Using the top X draw in more lines for the torches on either side of the figure.

Add more shading using a soft pencil. Start adding some decoration into the background torches. Don't forget to add the shadow below Adin. When you've finished rub out the working lines.

The Magic City

The Magic City of Tora is the chief city of Deltora's west, in the territory of the amethyst.
It was carved by magic from a marble mountain and is all of one piece—without crack or seam.
No evil can enter it and remain strong.

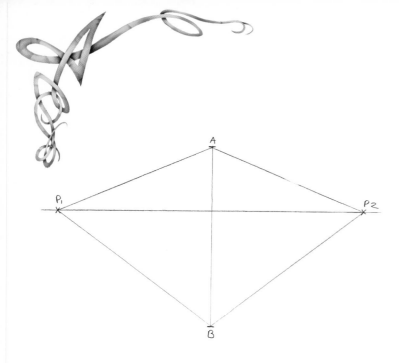

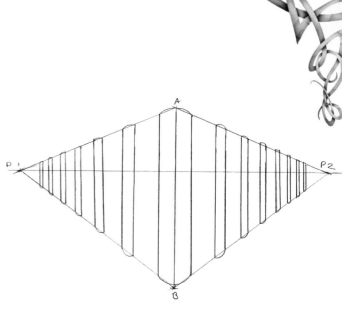

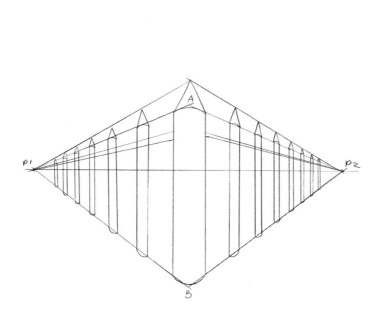

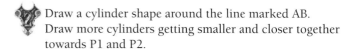

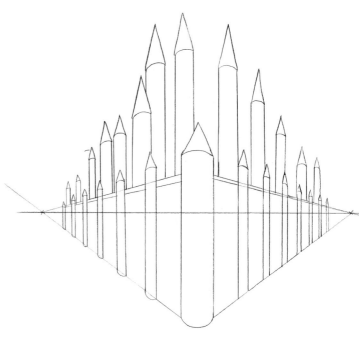

1 Draw a horizontal line and mark an X at each end: P1 and P2. In the center, draw a vertical line—make it longer below the horizontal line. Label the vertical line with A and B as shown. Rule lines from P1 and P2 to A and B to create a diamond shape.

2 Draw a cylinder shape around the line marked AB. Draw more cylinders getting smaller and closer together towards P1 and P2.

3 Draw a triangle on top of the first cylinder shape. Rule a line from the top of that triangle to P1 and P2. We can now draw triangles above all the cylinders just below this line to get the correct angle.

4 Rub out some of your working lines and draw more cylinders with triangle roofs above those you have already drawn. They can be as tall or as short as you like.

Rub out more of your working lines. Draw in more cylinders with triangular roofs behind—they will be smaller because they are further away. Add bridges and arches to join some of them together.

Add more detail like balconies, ornamental shapes, turrets and castle-like walls. Add an archway, windows and a door on the first main tower.

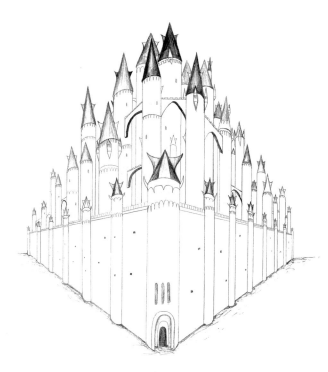

Start shading—the turret roofs first. The darkest parts will be inside the doorway and under the arches.

Draw in the ground and trees so the city is on top of a hill, with a path leading to the door. Give the marble walls some texture.

The Masked One

The evil being that was known as The Masked One lurked in a castle deep in the mountains near a place called Shadowgate. The Masked One was a Shadow Lord servant, and the guardian of the fearful creation called the Sister of the North.

1 Draw two arcs for the sleeves of the cloak and add a hood shape behind, joining them up.

2 Begin drawing the fingers with simple "sausage" shapes. Remember that the left hand is bigger as it reaches out to us. Start adding some snake shapes at the bottom of the figure.

3 Join the finger shapes to form the hands. Draw a mask shape behind the hands with a fold below it. Draw some more snakes with wide-open mouths. Make the ones in front larger.

4 Add some eyes and a slit for a mouth and add some more folds below the mask. Add detail to the snakes with lots of triangle shapes for fangs.

5 Draw in more snakes and folds in the robes.

6 Give the snakes a pattern—think of all the patterns that exist in nature. When shading, remember that the darkest parts are inside the sleeves.

Grey Guard

Grey Guards form the Shadow Lord's army. They are created in the Shadowlands in pods of ten. Each member of a pod looks exactly like his brothers. Grey Guards know no pity, and exist only to obey their master.

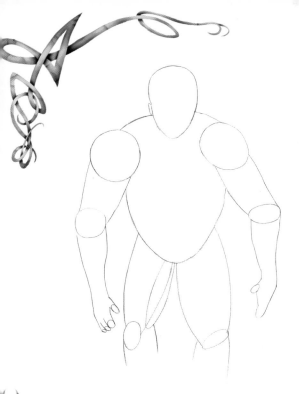

1 Evoke the size and bulky strength of the Grey Guard with a large frame using blocky shapes for the torso and head, but give him thin arms and legs. The oversized shoulders give him a slightly awkward look.

2 Start adding the helmet, shoulders, belt, blisters, and breastplate. Start outlining the features on the face.

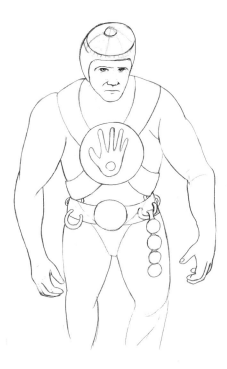

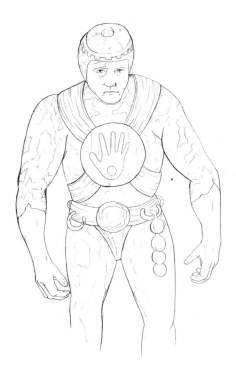

3 Clean up the working lines. Develop more detail in the face. Add the Shadow Lord sign and hooks on the belt.

4 Clean up the lines and add some texture to his worn clothes, and add shading where the shadows naturally fall to give depth to your drawing.

Adin Fighting a Vraal

1 Draw the figure of Adin holding a sword in an action pose. The Vraal is closer to us so draw it bigger. The Vraal's claw is the closest of all, so make it really big to create depth and add interest to your drawing.

2 Add a yellowish sky and gradually add some red at the top of the page. The sky will be the lightest part as it is farther away than anything else in your drawing.

Draw some raised swords, axes and banners along the horizon line to look like warriors fighting in the background. Keep them light because they are far off in the distance. My background is mostly red, the Shadow Lord's color. Too many colors in the background can be distracting from the main action.

3 Add more red to the sky and a darker brown over that to give depth and shape to the clouds. Add more fighting figures—with greater detail as they get closer, but don't clutter it too much at this stage.

4 Paint the purple cloak, gemstones (remember the order), dark hair, and boots—these will be the darkest parts of Adin. Start adding some gold into the sword handle. Draw some dragons and flying creatures in the sky.

Start adding some blue-gray tones to the metal of the breastplate and sword. For flesh tones I usually start with a yellow with a tiny amount of magenta mixed in.

Add darker shadows to the metal—remember the light source is normally from above. Be careful when you add dark colors as they are difficult to change if you make a mistake.

Add some brown with a hint of red into the shadows in the face—under the nose, and around the eyes and mouth.

Paint dark red inside the Vraal's mouth and around its wrinkled head. The red on the gums should be brighter than the red in the background to make them stand out. Mix some yellow and brown on the claws as well as behind the jaws.

Add shadow to the claws—darker at the bottom, light reflection along the top. Start coloring the Vraal's arm with yellow. Note lots of circle shapes running up to the shoulder.

 Continue the yellow over the body with a pattern a bit like crocodile skin.

Go over the top of the yellow with green, using slightly less of this color, and build up the patterns on the skin.

Add shadows around the scales, arm and along the tail as it gets further away.

Finally add a pattern to the Vraal. You can make this up or get ideas from nature. Deep sea fish are my favorite— they often communicate with other fish through their patterns. I think a Vraal might communicate danger!

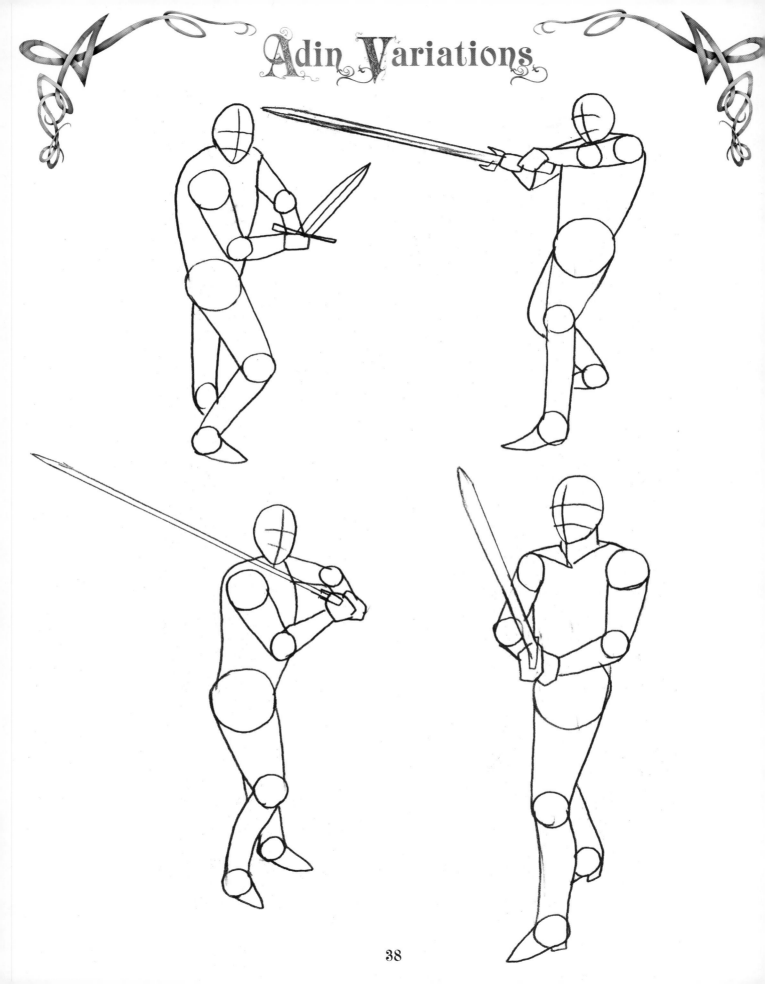

Adin Variations

Amethyst Dragon

Draw a large dragon with six smaller ones in the background. Add flames from the main dragon and a circle in the background for the moon.

This will be a nighttime scene to make the flames really stand out, so paint a dark background.

Give the background dragons a light wash in the colors of Deltora dragons—remember the colors of their underbellies reflect the color of the sky. The dragons at the top of your picture are reflecting the blue light of the moon, while the ones at the bottom have a hint of the purple flames. Add a light wash of color in the flames at the bottom of the picture. My main dragon is Veritas, the Amethyst Dragon, so my flames will be purple. Add some light texture into the moon.

Add a second darker layer over each dragon and add some colored flame from each one's mouth. Add a darker purple in the main flames—be careful not to add too much as the flames are very bright. Add some scales to the dragon. Think about the simple shapes that it is made of—for example, the arm is like a cylinder so the scales will twist around it.

 Add some light blue on the dragon's underbelly and under its wing. It will have a slight reflection from the moon, our primary light source, and from the flames, the secondary light source.

 Add shadows. Just under the neck will be the darkest area, where the head casts a shadow as the light comes from the flames. There is also some light coming from the moon, so the top of the dragon will be lighter.

 Paint around the scales with a light purple. Think about the light and what areas will be lighter and darker. Paint the dragon's spines and claws.

 Add a light purple to the dragon's head; leave the eyes and teeth white for now. Make the mouth dark as it is in shadow. Add some pink membrane around the mouth.

 Add some purple scales and a layer of darker purple over the top, thinking about the shadows and the shape of the head.

Add the darkest shadows to the head, including the eyes, which will have shadow at the top from the eyelid, and the teeth, which will have shadow from the gums. Add dark purples to the dragon's underbelly and the underside of the wing to reflect the dark background as well as the flames below.

As a finishing touch you might want to add background stars by flicking the bristles of a toothbrush lightly dipped in paint.